# Childhood Lore

*the collected poems*

Kate Gough

to the ones who cannot get out of bed.
to the ones who are told it is all in their head.
to the ones who stain their dresses red.
to the ones who sometimes wish they were dead.
May these poems bring peace, your dearest heart knows best.
May the pain soon cease. May you find true rest.

*(from Cottage in a Mirror)*

# Contents

*Trigger Warning*

*Childhood Lore explores the emotional, psychological, and physical land-scapes of girlhood and memory. The book contains references to childhood trauma, emotional neglect, sexual violence, and experiences of vulner-ability and harm. Several poems address both mental and physical health struggles, including chronic illness, pain, anxiety, and dissociation, as well as the lasting impact of formative relationships. Readers who are sensitive to these themes may wish to approach the collection with care.*

## Publisher's Note

Kate Gough writes with the ferocity of someone who remembers everything: the dolls, the fairy tales, the secret rules, the quiet violences that shaped us long before we had language for any of it. These poems do not pretend. They do not flinch. They walk straight into the plastic worlds we were handed as children and illuminate them from the inside, showing both the tenderness and the ruin.

As a publisher, you always hope to encounter a voice that feels necessary — not because it is loud, but because it is honest. Kate has written poems that honour the little selves we built out of paper, thread, and imagination; the girls who survived on lore and instinct; the ones still living inside us, rearranging the dollhouse furniture, trying to make sense of the world.

This is a collection stitched together with sincerity, myth, rebellion, and a kind of reverence for the child who once believed in everything. It is also a reckoning — with girlhood, with loss, with the stories that shaped us and the ones that saved us.

I am proud of Kate for the courage and precision threaded into every poem. And I am grateful for the reminder that the worlds we built as children were never frivolous. They were blueprints. They were survival. They were prophecy.

May this collection find the readers who need it most.

— Rebecca Calles Rijsdijk
Publisher, *Sunday Mornings at the River*

## Foreword

This collection is folklore unlike any you have read before.
This is an honest fairytale that makes no effort to hide the raw,
bloodied edges of flesh it takes to build your own happy
ending.

*"So how can we wish her a happily ever after, when she is being offered
with a red ribbon around her neck?"*

This is a story about dangerous little girls who grow into
women that wield their pain like weapons, their clothing
stained — from fruit or blood, we can't tell — as they fight
through a dark forest of sickly trees and dead corpses, flailing
in agony and screaming with rage. Gough refers to strong
women of the past who suffered greatly — Agatha,
Persephone, Ophelia, Joan, Frida, and more — and write
through their eyes, with their tongues, across the wide expanse
of womanhood and how women suffer.

The poems within juxtapose the domestic idea of a woman
with the disturbing realities of it, the constant fight between
conforming and losing your goddamned mind, all while tinged
with the stale taste of sickness as the author delves into her
experiences with chronic illness. Gough paints beautiful images
of suffering as a reminder that suffering is in fact not beautiful
at all.

*"All you want is to shut me up. I just wait. I get to suffer first."*

The poems dance between lily-white rage and a soft kind of
strength, stretching from the innocence of girlhood to the
weight of being a modern woman in a world that prefers girls

that are quiet and tame. This collection fights these expectations with dark, confessional tales about the honest experience of being a woman; a young woman, a sick woman, a corpse on the cottage floor.

*"Never have they seen a corpse so chic."*

I know you will enjoy it as much as I did.

**Salem Paige**

*Kate Gough*

## Prologue

Kneeling at the hearth, she does anything but pray,
for the lovely lore
tells the tale of the familiar beasts, the monster kings,
the toadstools she took to end her life twice…
the little girl's first lesson is that her worth is dangerous.
Petal pollen stains her red dress—her favourite colour;
it hides the blood.
Wild men say that only fools sin.
Wild women say that only men give in.
She is so sick of the medicine
that seeps through her skin to make her feel not better,
but not worse.
Somewhere in the middle, her eyes crimson
from the lack of restorative sleep,
flower's fog keeps her spirits up,
and girlhood keeps her in trouble.

*Cottage in a Mirror*

### Like Esther

I wish to be one
with the gifts I am given,
to thwart the evils of apples,
use my beauty,
or my youth,
or some other wasted vanity,
to sacrifice myself for the good of all.
Like Esther of old, or little Laura
running all night long to warn the loyal,
I would use my charms, wit, and grit
to prevent annihilation.
No matter the battle,
I want to be brave
like they were.
I want to be
a bridge, a queen,
a welcomer of the dawn.
I want to rule,
to lead and say something loudly.
I gnash my teeth
as I charm her with the last my body can muster.
Prostitute of pain, I ask for the secret.
I cry for a voice.
The voice that answers is one of a woman.


She answers:


LOOK UP! The moon does not answer to the earth,
but it thrives in the shadows, keeping the tides at bay.
I must live silently in order to be brave.

I speak only in poems and riddles
in order to be understood.
One day, they'll find the poetry books
and wonder,
"Who was she really?"
and I'll be at peace.

## Saint Agatha

I read the story of Saint Agatha,
and mind you, I am no saint.
But when I read about her tragedy,
I am reminded of the love she had before her death.
I see you othering those you deem unworthy of love,
and I am reminded of Agatha, and of Catherine, of Joan,
and of all the other saints who gave their lives to love.

You sit in your ivory tower and laugh at those who are next.
You think you deserve better.
They will come for you just the same.
You let them treat one of us like this—
they do not see the difference between us and them.
You are not protected by your hate.

You scream
that I enjoy being a victim.
Otherwise, why have I not healed by now?

My voice has changed since the day he raped me.
It is hoarse from the acidic milk
that coats my lungs.

My body has changed.
It is lined with ulcerative pain, inflamed.
Like Agatha, I am tortured, forever ill.

My mind has changed.
It is paranoid and triggered by any violence,
even when separated by a black mirror.

There are bruised fingerprints on my heart, and despite them,
I still crave love. I need to love. I pry off hatred's bitter hold,
and I hope I will forever remain me.

I am no saint. I am no tragedy.
I am a lover in a world of hate.
And I need friends.

## Pretty, the Fruit of Snakes

Cut with hands of lace,
she was pretty.
That was enough to be saved,
she thought.
Saddened, she didn't know better.
Snake coiled around her neck,
she was dying,
strangled—better not to scream,
she thought.
Feather and flower in hand,
she was mourning,
no one was coming to save her like
she thought.
Abandoned,
she didn't know better.
Fruit of the tree,
she is eating.
It is enough to be tender.
Apricot juice stains white cotton,
the better it is to know
how it tastes.

*Kate Gough*

**View From the Window**

View from the window: scratchy surface,
like your beard growing in,
wild and untamed in a winter's city
of barren trees, pretty
like skeleton roots.
On the terrace, nothing but snow.
View from the window: glassy surface,
like your eyes,
sunken in,
soaked to the bone
in a marshy swale
of icky heart, pale
like a lost tooth.
See your chaos,
hermit and glow.

## I Crave

*I crave …*

peace of mind,
my grandmother's old backyard,
a breath of sea air,
a chamomile tea with honey,
relief from the chronic pain,
a yam torte from my favourite restaurant,
rest from the constant fatigue,
films that make me laugh and cry,
something challenging to occupy my restless mind,
a catharsis,
refuge from the dreaded hospital stays,
old books that tell me things that still ring true,
freedom for the oppressed,
freedom for the rest,
a body that actually works,
peace on earth.

*Kate Gough*

## Grim and Bear It

Art smushed into our hands like cranberries,
we roast in the wintertime.
Painted in resin, a ceramic vase
keeps the dead roses together.
You think they are lovely, even though they droop.
That which rots is birth to new.
Dig through the mud,
archaeologist of beautiful, twisted things:
a skull, the classic tattoo, ink carved into flesh...
I guess the arts are morbid too.
Take a bite—the forest floor spits out specks
of dirt and toadstool.
The charm of poison kills the curiouser.
Not in death, but in life is searing pain—
the ugliness and horror
of the very first thing we ever see: new birth.

## Persephone

I was tempted by pomegranate seeds,
and now autumn and winter are barren.
My mother searched for me as the months passed—
heart traded for heart, I was a prisoner to the underworld;
she was great with child. And so we withered.
Persimmon-coloured leaves fall to my feet
as I dance in the dress I was making before I was taken.
They call me the angry one; I hate them for making me so.
But when my mother sings me her song, I am one
with the seasons. I am fierce.
I am found.

## Ophelia

*Ugly delicious—*
is there a term like that for people?
A feast made by the gentle of hand, homemade—
is that what we aim for?
A wolf in sheep's wool clothing, perhaps?
The darling, she gifted daisy, fennel, and rue
to the man who couldn't hide for long,
a beautiful bouquet to mask hate's pungent reeking.
Had she gifted a wasp's nest,
would she still be remembered
as a lady lost to madness?

*Ugly delicious—*
the grotesque cached behind her own
rotting corpse.
In the lake, she was painted as beautiful.
She choked and suffered,
burned through her lungs;
she went limp, and bloated, and rotted to death.
Yet they remember her madness as delicate.

Wreathed in wildflowers, she was the original queen,
the one who deserved so much better.
Ugly delicious—complex, as in a pretty monster.
What the water did to her—
had she not been gently strewn,
would she still be remembered
as a lady lost to madness?

### A Letter to My 13-Year-Old Self

*Dear 13-year-old Kate,*

Please know, before anything else,
you are happier than you've ever been.
I know you are afraid.
I know you are completely consumed by your fear.
I'm sorry you were alone when you needed someone like me
to guide you.
I'm sorry you didn't know any better. I'm sorry you had to
learn the hard way.

Please know that you will find a certain type of peace.
It will be a quiet peace.
You will have to work hard to keep that peace within.
Remember to find a friend in nature, and in the little things.
Go on walks by the river. Go on picnics. Bake and cook and be
nourished. Knit that scarf you still haven't finished. Make as
much bad art as you can. Write poems, and write for yourself,
and write to cope, and write, write, write.

You will find your spark in the warmth of life. Be cozy.
Romanticize the little things—the honey jars and the poetry
books, the studious autumn, the rabbit tattoos. You will be so
loved, by such beautiful people. You are beautiful. You might
not feel beautiful, but you are so dear to so many. You will find
people who will never think you are a burden.

Dearest Kate, you will learn your worth, and you will learn to
love yourself. I hope you trust the universe a little more. There

are good things ahead. Pace yourself, slow down, and enjoy your time here. We only have so little left.
Be patient, be kind, and be soft.
I love you.

## The Circus Master

While the carousel horses gallop through her mind,
sugarplum miseries await her,
turning left at the end of dreamland
to an elephant graveyard
where the games are on.

She is a circus master
to the drum of her heartbeat.
A performance of pain
to the chucklers and groaners—
they chuck rotten tomatoes at her chin.

She is the main event, the golden goddess
in a tiara of jewels;
she is the one they all came to see.
She falls ill in love,
and they love to marvel at the stars.

Tonight the show must go on!
She takes the pills
and fills her cup with tonic;
she is the star of the greatest show on earth.

The applause is a candle going out in a forest.

## The Dancer

Cold bathroom floor. She is awake.
She can't move. Pale, sickly legs can't lift up
the caged body.
Ice-cold feet,
a ballerina dancer.
Bandaged and beaten,
she can't dance on her feet
when she's cold.

Broken-in shoes
are the ones
she burned for
their sweet spice—
fire over ice,
naught or nice,
it doesn't matter.

Cold bathroom floors do not discriminate.

## Sorry for the Sick

Prickly shame
of rose thorns,
finger drips blood
into glass.

Weeds in my garden,
plaque in my mouth,
I blame myself in poems.
Charge cast to punish us
for all I cannot control.

Opioid and water—
sick comes back up,
and I blame myself.

Sorry for the sick—
I lie; I want to be better, so I try,
my stomach churning.

Sorry for the sick—
I fake; my heart breaks to look healthy,
I'm still learning.

Sorry for the sick—
I quake; my lip shakes in the flame
of inside burning.

*Kate Gough*

## Burgundy Stain on a White Dress

Tender is the fright
of the girl; burgundy stains
the crisp white dress
she wears when she is nervous.

Pin a note on her chest
to warn the others.
Psssst... she is scared.
They mean no harm—hush now.

But the sticky residue of scars trickles,
drop by drop, into the dull red wine.
Beautiful, the god-damned fools,
can't help but gawk and scoff
at the stained dress
and her fake smile.

## Love and Other Bargains

You praise my wholeness.
It'd be better if I died a virgin
than lived a happy life of seeing red.
You value naivety as if it's a gem,
but I'm afraid, darling, I'm only gold-plated.

You bathe me in incense; you worship me for not
knowing how to please you.
It's easier to tie me up that way.
Better to tease you.
Burn me at the stake,
turn me on the wheel, swallow me whole.
My death is holy—
or so they say—if only
I remained pure
and said no.

You torture me for my consent, and if I keep my virtue,
I am to be a saint
and loved forever.
What a bargain.

Little girls will pray to me and ask how I kept my
legs shut;
they'll beg for my pardon.
But to die young—
it is the price for eternal, perpetual virginity.
What a bargain.

## Leech

You were the one who told me
I need to feel—
the bandages
on my fingers,
the blood
from the bile
in my own mouth.

To feel it is to hate it;
please don't convince me otherwise.
You slather pseudo-salve
on my wounds and tell me
to love the sunburn inside.

Parasitic leech it is—I lash out,
and I am sorry.
I am trying not to be sorry so often.

You were the one who told me
I need to breathe—
the wind
in my tense lungs.
You find something
as basic as breathing beautiful.

How do you see me?
Parasitic leech it is—loneliness...
I am sorry.
I am trying not to be sorry so often.

## Red Cherry

Cherry-picking red-flavoured truth
to hide the stain of bloodlust.
Rose-coloured glasses frame the eyes,
the doctrine, and the lies—
like pretty candy on a silver spoon,
remember to steal from the baby.

An acquired taste for nuance
is a warrant for shame.
Stitch her skin with a red A,
refund her virtue one-way ticket
to the damned.

Beautiful—it's either all true, or all false.
No redemption for the ones they call sluts.

## The Prisoner to Looking Similar

The dark prison I used to sustain around me
was built on long black lashes,
tiny cinched waists,
and ruby red lips…
A glow-up world
where no light was to be found.

I was a prisoner to the pain,
to the fifty pounds I gained,
to the clothes that wouldn't fit,
and the mirrors that reflected it.
I was ugly, and that meant
the world smugly
told me that I did not belong.

I want to tell that girl who sucked in her stomach
enough that it hurt,
that girl who counted every calorie—
from celery to yogurt—
that girl who cried the day
she was told her body
was unable to lose weight
due to her illness,

I want to tell her that
she doesn't need to perform pretty.
She is good enough; she is clever and witty,
she is loving, she is kind, she is silly,
she has a beautiful mind.

She doesn't need to be a prisoner
to wearing lipstick and looking similar.

# Life Sentence

Punctuate a life sentence of pain
with a flourish of the sword.
It will not end.

Birthday, wedding day, funeral—
to place on my shoulders
a cloak: burn, itch, ache,
and ask me why I do not take it off?

Punctuate a life sentence of pain
by giving me the last word.

## Blood Orange

Blood-orange guts
rake her skin open
to bare a citrusy stain of a girl.

Heart cut in two—
the most important meal of the day.
Forgive her innards
for their pungent essence.

Cleanse with a soapy lemon bar, air-dry outside,
lay her out over blue and white shutters.
Pulp and seeds—let the tartness of sin
ease the girl soaked in orange juice's nectar.

She cries over the breakfast she couldn't finish.

## Cottage in a Mirror

Little blue door,
open up,
and see through.

Vulnerable—every blemish bright
in the mirrored frame of a poem.
I can go out in the rain;
stay inside another day and I will fall short—
ho-hum and a sigh.

Spice and sugar,
and a little bit of vigour—
cottage life smells of cider and wool.

Look at me and see
a quiet life; forget the pain,
so tired and sore,
just another spoonful
of mirror shards and fear.

But I am home, and warmth is near.

## Heart-Shaped

Break me open;
inside the heart-shaped box is secret and myth,
on the tip of the tongue—talk and listen to the broken
pieces, skin and pith.

Love, as a word,
means more than the proverb of giver in war—lost
in potion of spice and herb, rune spoken and stirred;
drown my heart, uncrossed.

Inside the organ,
the blood pumps the fist down the throat
where I was kissed.

Out of boredom,
you loved me in quotes.

*Kate Gough*

## The Heroines and the Dragon

Heroine, a vision in cotton,
place the lavender bushel beneath the firewood.
The flames are enough for the scent to burn.
We smell the smoke—a call to action.

Women, we are burgundy-blooded and lily-white,
laced into our corsets.
We are gutted by the evils of man.
Milk rather than blood flows from her neck.

Catherine of Alexandria, dear, we come to her—
and her silver tongue; let us weep with her sisters,
until the tears melt the candle wax.

Swallowed whole by the dragon himself,
Margaret of Antioch, dear, we come to her—
and her golden cross; let us kiss her wounds,
until our lips have been stained with blood.

Burnt at the stake with the fire of the dragon,
Joan of Arc, dear, we come in our suits of armour
to slay him who martyred the heroines of old.

Heroines, the virgin martyrs—these three saints
of milk, blood, and fire
hold truth
in dreams, in sincerity,
and in final breath.

## Watercolour Band-Aids

A blistered touch,
replace fingers with twiggy daisies.
Watercolour paint and Band-Aids plaster skin.
Play Clair de lune from the next room—you will heal
soon.

Radio says your generation is weak.
Back in their day,
they cut up their hands and
soaked them in lemon juice.

What a bright red wound to emulate!
Let their pride to suffer define them—
but not you.

## Frida's Bathwater

Taste her sweat, Frida—like bathwater,
bitter and filthy of mind; naivety was her drink of
choice. Took a sip, but the damned pain would swim.
Grey, watery thighs—she was an island,
a small skeleton resting upon a hill.

Duality of the body she lost and the body she had; she
would rot, rest soon. Naked as she floated, I looked into
her eyes, my hands wrapped around her neck.
Seashells cupping her breasts—they were full of bullet
holes. Water drunk like erotica, a painting left for dead.
Sweat, soap, and metal—she was what the water gave me.

Thank the saints in this calamity;
save me from my body!
It pains me, as my feet cannot touch the ground
to feel the sand.

Retablos of Mother Mary tell me she had a great smile.
The sea smells like her, I told myself.
I grew up a virgin to Mother without pause...
Thank the saints in this sea storm; save her from the
womb! I would pray.

Roots from my wrists—I grew
familiar with blooming.
Folklore of an ancient tree; from the trunk
grows a ribbon.

I used to tie up my tresses every morning.
Now I wear a mask to hide my face, but I dance.
I dance into the night with the other women.
We are all so young, virtue is tight, but my hair is looser.

Like bathwater—lather and dirt caked on skin; sin is a
sip. Damned pain—God damn it—as the Mother
cleans her child, she weeps.
A child ready for bed.

Thank the fates. Thank the fates.

## Eat Me

Ice melts in the mouth; I am metallic in the sun.
Hot to the touch—the doctors even say so.
Where does the heat go? Through my skin like sweat,
or steaming through my ears
like a moustachioed villain?

Maybe it's where my blood goes,
as I haemorrhage on the bed,
the heat sticking to the linoleum floor.
Red ribbons tie my hands to the IV;
skeleton friends lie above me.
They see me naked, but intimate is not the word
I would use.

Anatomically, I am a body—nothing special.
Memory, the heart—splay my innards onto the grass
and throw my torn dress to the sea.

Heartbreak would never be preferable,
not to me. I have a hunger—for fullness,
for a plump figure and a bookmarked mind.
To break a piece of me is to devour me
and spit me out with your wine;
I am to be consumed fully.

*Eat me.*

*The Maiden in the Tower*

### A Letter to the Chronically Ill

They don't warn you
about the plastic pill bottles in the cupboard,
the ones that twist off—the child-safe kind, the ones you're
supposed to take every day…

They don't warn you
that it will get harder to open the bottle.
That your hands will shake, unable to push down with enough
pressure to twist off the cap.
They don't warn you that this is a side effect.
They don't warn you on the bottle that the chemicals within
might make everything worse. Or unbelievably better. It's a
gamble of flesh.

They don't warn you that you will be their puffy-cheeked
lab rat,
devouring poison cheese
as they write down indecipherable notes.

You are alone when you wonder,
Why isn't it helping?
Is it somehow making it worse?
How could it get any worse?

They don't warn you when you get sick, that this is it.
Pain is a bitter pill to swallow, but hope coats it in sugary
needles,
stabbing you as it goes down.
They don't warn you
that hope will choke you.

You are alone when you wonder,
Why aren't I getting better?
What did I do wrong?
What is wrong with me?

They don't warn you that you will be misunderstood.
They don't warn you that you will mourn your health and your future.
They don't warn you that you will give up hope.
They don't warn you that you will feel less than human.

But they also don't let you in on a secret kept close
by those burned, bruised, and blistered…

Giving up hope will set you free.
You do not need to be like them.
You do not need to hold on to a pain-free future.
You do not need to grasp the hope that you will get better.
You are allowed to let go of the life of the abled;
you are allowed to be chronically ill.

For all the warnings I was never given, I warn you now:
People will misunderstand.
People will think you are faking.
People will make you think it's all in your head.

You are not to blame.
It is not your fault you are sick.
It is not in your head. It is real, and it is so very, very painful.
You deserve relief and rest. You deserve the right medication.
You deserve accommodation and respect.

CHILDHOOD LORE

You are ill,
and you are not to blame.

## Poppy, Fresh as Blood

Poppies in a vase, red—fresh as blood on a ceramic curve,
she was an angel; they called her a fighter,
as she slept in the hospital bed.

They could not see inside—
inflamed bubbles under her pale skin;
they were hot like ash, her face waxen under the harsh light.

She was red, poppy red; remember her as she tossed,
she turned,
she was hot pain in a colourless body.
Sallow cheeks, pinched to please them.

Poppy red—fresh as blood on an anaemic curve,
she was an angel, a fighter…
They forget her when the flowers have dried.

## Coping Hollow

Crunching spine,
chaos of mine,
I bellyache and whimper
at a mere touch to the nape of my neck.

The bottom of the vertebrae carves its initials
like lovers' names into bark.
A thousand and one poems about the pain,
I never say its name again.
It doesn't deserve the attention.

But I need to cathartically wail.
For this is my little spot of earth to scream on.
And I ache
in this dirt- and worm-encrusted grave.

I have nowhere to turn.
No room in the sick house.
I must bear it like the rain, like gloom on my eyelashes.

Bleeding mind,
chaos of mine,
I will wail as you jab me with cold, sterile tools.
In this coping hollow,
rest will hopefully follow.

I ache.

## Crush, Break, Bruise, Chew

Crush me like the powdery drug,
crush me like a flittering bug.

Break me like a beating heart,
break me before I can even start
to heal.
But I will heal.

Bruise me like a delicate peach,
bruise me like a thirsty leech.

Chew me like a savoury feast.
Chew me out like a robotic beast who
hates to feel.
But I will feel.

### Winter's Curse

Winter's curse
coats the eyelashes with wet frost,
a rotting gut, a bloody anus, and deep malaise.
That's just the tip of the iceberg.

Beneath the cold sea
thrashes a blue, living corpse
who breathes through a machine,
and can't help but see
the pain in everyone's eyes
as they meet.

Winter's curse
is knowing that no matter how warmly you dress,
your bones will shudder from the cold.

Winter's curse
is breathing ice with a mask on,
being ridiculed for wearing chainmail
as they stab you in the back.

Winter's curse
is feeling the weight of the world on your shoulders,
and being scorned for not pushing the boulder
up the hill once again—for the thousandth time—
in this damned plane of purgatory.

The eyes of the helpers—
they watch with pity; they resent you
for not being helped

the way you should be.
The shrugs of the healers—
they laugh 'cause it's a regular Tuesday,
as they tell you they've failed you
and decide not to help.

The worst of the curse
is they tell you to be grateful
as you writhe in the storm,
blizzard blinding, blessings binding—
you are nothing if you are not a cry in the wind.

## Fool's Label

Useful—a fool's label,
they want to be used by the world like a napkin on a wet chin,
abused by the world like a woman who has supposedly sinned.
They want to be chewed, spat, and bile dribbled down the
front of the bib of the baby
that is crying—crying for us to feed her—
all the while we are burnt out
and we can't tell what is useful and what is a noose…

What do you call it
when you sleep—
is it not useful to rest?

What do you call it
when you vent—
is it not useful to heal?

What do you call it
when you cry—
is it not useful to feel?

Useful—a tool to feel needed,
they want to be loved by the world like a warm meal around
the hearth,
beloved by the world like the sunset—we watch it like
television.
They want to be seen, heard, and loved as they fail
and they try,
try again.

## The Maiden in the Tower

The maiden in the tower,
she lives.
She loves.

Her love and life mean the same
as the knight who endures deserts and sails oceans
to be with her.

Quiet is her love, but from the tower
she beckons like a lighthouse:
"Come to me,
and be free.

For I am not the one in shackles, though I am faint.
I am the forces of the universe,
I am illness and health,
I am life and death,
I am love and loss.

I send you letters, write songs
for when you find me,
and I will sing them to you,
and you will weep.

I am a castle unto myself,
and I am the one you cannot live without."

The maiden in the tower—sick though she may be—
she is revolutionary.
She is the one they all want to see.

## Bedsheet Place I Rest In

Sticky skin to the bedsheet place
you rest—if you can call it that.
Toss and turn for one second of relief;
bleeding inside, you stink of sweat and sick.

You peel your eyelids open to an empty stucco ceiling.
Minutes—each hour passes slowly,
sickly sweet like molasses; your teeth start to take up space in
your head.

No one tells you when
you are pronounced ill, like a hollow yawp…
that apart from the pain, the fatigue, and the thousand other
symptoms,
you will suffer the most
from idle thought.

Trickling down your thought canal
go the tears and other liquids.

You are sick—now what?
You wait. You don't die yet.
You wait, and you lie in rest.
If you can call it that.

## Candlelight

Moon river and candlelight, shadowed tip of the nose—
I lament. I am never quiet enough for my liking.
The temperamental fierceness of a storm,
its chronic waves, a sea of moor and salt, ulcer-lined
fragility. It is supernatural, the torment my body endures.

And I am so very tired.
Living cadaver, candlelit vigil for my own fibres.
I light the wax to feel warm, and I open my eyes to a soft glow.

Death will not allow me safety from fluorescent light.
In life, I must live in candlelight.

## I Am Not Getting Any Younger

Sinking in, my feet flail to the floor,
crunch—underneath are bones, leaves, and blood.
I am begging you to take my hand, lift me up;
I cannot stand up, not anymore.

Do you know what it feels like to lose your own steps?
I am only meat and bone. I should have known
how precious this vessel is. I only had twenty good
years—most get fifty.
And to be strong is to be the poster child of not being bitter.

I am bitter. And they say:
Just wait. It will get worse.
Existential promise of pain—thanks for the reason not to
complain.
All you want is to shut me up.
Just wait. I get to suffer first.

Sinking in, my feet flail to the floor,
crackle, the skin flakes.
I am begging you to understand.
I am not getting any younger.

### Grieve, Health Is Gone

*Grieve,*
health is gone.
You cannot breathe the way you used to.
You are told you look well,
after ulcers eat your own guts.
You feel like you have to hide it.
But you cannot go on with your day the way you used to.

*Grieve,*
you feel guilty about rest.
They say you're overreacting
when you tell them you just can't do it again.
You cannot eat the way you used to.
Wondering if you'll ever get better,
you start to see it as a new normal,
until a new diagnosis shatters it all to pieces.
You cannot afford anything anymore, and the treatment costs
keep piling up.
You cannot live the way you used to.

*Grieve,*
you feel afraid of new symptoms.
You feel afraid of overdoing it, and suffering later.
You wonder how anyone could ever love you like this.
They think you're a burden, even the ones who care.
You cannot love the way you used to.

*Grieve,*
you accept it's not going to get better.
You wish everyone else would accept it too.
You feel burnt out by their doubting gaze.
But you no longer feel guilty for doing it your way.

Health is gone, but you are here.
Release the future, the doubt, the shame.
You are here now.

## Magnify Me

Magnify me. Reveal my breathing patterns at night.
They can't be captured. The machine they strapped to my face
is denied to me by the same people who hate to wear a flimsy
piece of fabric.
They rioted over cotton. I will die over a technicality.

When I get the letter in the mail
and find out they don't care enough for me to breathe in my
sleep,
I weep.
And I refuse to sleep.

Magnify me. Reveal the tears, the snores, the fears.
And bite me as I keep a tally.

## I Sleep Like the Sick Do

The skin, too loud,
the wind, too bitter,
the blankets, too wet—
I feel it all.
I gag. I flinch. I wince. I stall.

Nothing and everything all at once,
a sensory prison—how long a sentence
must I write
until I fall
asleep?

1:46 a.m., doom-scrolling, leg shaking,
sweat sticky, sheets pasted to me.
Fifty times an hour I restart the cycle,
fifty times an hour I struggle to sleep,
fifty times an hour I cannot breathe.

The mind, too numb,
the adrenaline, less so.
The body, too ill
to heal at all.
I cry. I toss. I turn. I scroll.

Nothing and everything all at once,
a sensory prison—how long a poem
must I write
until I fall
asleep?
A 2:00 a.m. thought:

If universal is the poet and the bed,
why aren't there libraries dedicated to illness?
What is more human than to lose our health?

Suffer like the poets do.
Asleep, I write like the dreamers do.
Dead, I sleep like the sick do.

*Kate Gough*

## ER Static

Freckle of pain in the eye,
pat the skin to pull blood,
the veins are spider-bitten,
tamed by needles and tape,
pain pills, and a mocking moan
from behind the curtain.

Cotton gown bare—prod and poke
me until tears stick to my mask.
Fluorescent lights and bottles of urine,
I am not a human here. I shouldn't vomit.

*I am female, born in August.*

Been here over seven times in the last year.
TV scratch, scream, and morphine—
it's a place you hope you'll never be.
Broken, moan and sick, so many sorrys.

Waiting is a pastime for the wounded, but goddamn,
if you make her wait, she'll pounce, and be turned back,
making us listen to the bitching—mutter it quieter, will you?

The air is tense, like the nerves in my back—surgery next,
come back a few days later, it's burning. Never gives you peace.

Emergency room static—
it's a place you hope you'll never be.
For more than four hours.
Make that nine.

Seven days, and you're out, and you are a shell.
Scooped out of a net, you cry, but they hush you.
You say sorry when you scream.
They look down at your wrist and ask you your birthday.

*I am female, born in August.*

## Lot's Wife Deserved a Name

*"You don't really live, do you?"*
For to live is to move quickly,
without looking back,
lest a pillar of salt blind the eyes.

Eyes salted must be flushed.
Colons bloodied must be replaced.
Bodies broken must be healed—
and if they cannot be,
then swiftly erase them from mind.

You erase my life:
the red wine and bread,
the art and the talking—all that talking.
You erase me from my life without a thought.

You take your health for granted,
as if your lungs are worthy of air more than mine
because they can function without medicine.

I am alive, though I cannot run like you do.
I am alive, though I cannot work like you do.
I am alive, though I cannot shit like you do.

I am worthy to be alive.
I will not keep up with your living.

Look back, behind you.
You've forgotten me.
Pillar of salt—hey, what a gritty view.

*Kate Gough*

## We Won't Forget It

We light the insides of the dollhouse
with string lights and candles
to distract us from the fire in our own front yards.

But forget that.
Red is the colour of
rosy cheer,
a time for fir trees and wet noses.

We do what we can as the world gets colder;
a warmth was lost when we started hiding in October.
We can't forget that.

Red is the colour of
blood lost,
a time for too much hate,
a time for love at a cost.

You watch us in our warm homes, bitter you can't leave
the home—the hell—you have created.

As we wait patiently, we light ourselves
red with love, with hate, and with blood.

Your hate was terminal.
We won't forget that.

## Jane

I was a girl, fifteen in August.
I read *Jane Eyre* as if it were a diary entry—cliché, I know,
but I was only fourteen.
You were a boy. You smoked cigarettes.
You couldn't run a mile without needing rest.
What you said about us girls, I thought it was idle gossip.
But then again, red flags only exist to mock.

I was just a girl, you were just a boy—how could I tell them
what you did to me? What boys do when they are angry?
I would not learn the word incel until five years later,
but a label would not have saved me.
Red pills and red flags do not stop the blood from staining the
bathroom floor.

On the bus ride home I read Jane Eyre as if she was
whispering to me—
cliché, I know, but I was only fourteen.

"Do you know where the wicked go after death?"
"They go to hell."
"What must you do to avoid it?"
"I must keep in good health and not die."

I remember the promise I made to not kill myself.

Red pills, red flags, and red fire do not stop the heart
from pumping.
Red comes at night, but at least my wounds have
stopped bleeding.

I remember my promise as I read Brontë again, the burning shame of being
not quite fifteen. I don't remember as much of the pain these days,
but to write is to heal, and to love is to be like Jane.

## Janes That I Feel

I want to stay soft around my crude edges,
that broke their way from mountainsides
into flesh and blood, wombs erupted rock.
I want to be delicate.

But not in a fragile way. In a soft kind of strength.
I don't know what it looks like—only what it feels like.
Like red, mushy heartbeats after feeling true connection.
Like staying true to the inner cricket's orchestra—its
conscience
is on the loud side, but a soft kind of loud, chocolatey and rich.

I don't want to be cold, callous, and apathetic. I want to care.
I don't want brute force or cynicism. I want maximalist love.
I want to be a forceful nature of the windy moors, of the Janes
that feel,
rather than the Janes that repress their true love.

I want to live with more trust.
I am so fearful of pain, and I've earned it.
But I want to stay soft, whilst chronically wounded.
I want to be like the little one I used to be.

*Dollhouse Downfall*

## Fake Plastic Dream

I fell from the balcony,
but it was okay—the child
caught me in her stupor of play.

I watch her grow, cry, bruise, bite, and bleed.
I watch her grow up; a bittersweet crocodile
follows us as we tick tick tick away to Neverland.
As he follows, we never age, but she begins to fade—
cheeks sallow with hunger, she emulates
the fake plastic dream,
the doll with the flat feet cannot flex.

Years of restriction, counting and pinching,
hair loss and sick—she wanted to be like me.
But I am only a toy.

The fake plastic dream
will never feel skin on skin, the sound of rain,
the ever-ephemeral smell of petrichor in her red lungs.
I can sit in glitter and gloss, stuck in the narrative
a child can only make up.

Dollhouse lore—coat me in sincerity and push me down the throat
like a sugar-coated pill.
Make her believe in the fairytales, the tea-party truths.

A tale as old as time—let me go and let her eat,
for we all need to grow up sometime. Please,

be gentle; she only knows how to cope when
we are pretending.

## Cradle Me

It used to be so sweet.
The way you used to sing to me.
When I woke up, you'd smile at me.
You'd pick me up and cradle my head.
You'd hush my tears and sing me a melody.

I haven't slept for weeks.
I crave the soft place I used to sleep—
· the tender bosom, crested gently.
I wonder how long it's been
since I was actually asleep.

The bitter bind of pain
that accompanies this bag of bones—
it creaks and cries out
when it can no longer breathe—

You used to put me above all else.
You used to make me feel like no harm could fall upon me.
When I think about it, I can't help but weep.
The way I used to think I was safe.

It used to be so sweet.

## Mama, a Little Girl Too

Mama—she used to be a little girl too.
She knew what I knew at that age.

Girlhood: milkmaid braids and diet pills,
sugar and spice and everything nice,
blood on silk, spark of hate, disdain for glitter
and a passion for blood.
Women—kick us while we're down; we are all already bleeding.

She used to hate the colour pink
because it meant she was not like the cool girls
whom the men pit her against. It's not a competition—
it's just a colour. Pretty as a sunset, but pink hues
are not the only shade of girlhood.

Mama, when she was little,
she would make mud pies in the garden.
Provide for us, even as a child—she is a nurturer.
Give her a baby doll; let nature do the rest.

But she felt lost, looking into the blue glass eyes of the doll;
she couldn't help but wonder,
*How do I give up myself—give it all to baby?*
*How do mamas do it?*

Mamas—they used to be little girls too,
who would wince when the boys tugged at their braids at
school,
who would shudder at the catatonic catcalling from the
trenches,

who would rather die than let her body be degraded by the man in charge.

She dropped the baby doll into the wet dirt.

## Mother Bear

Look into
every car window, every black surface that reflects
my pale body back at me.
Spiderweb scars on my stomach,
a lost look on my face.

Mirrors, feed into my fears—
I wished more than anything
that I could live without being seen.

That lens, that monster, a bear that had been ingrained
inside—
it left its marks, clawing and scratching at my strings.
Grotesque, I thought, as I looked in the mirror.
Every scar, I thought, was a punishment.

They said that silencing the outer voices would change
things…
It did, but it didn't undo what I had been told,
what I had said to myself
for the last twenty-seven years.

Every mirror was an enemy.
Every tear was a memory.

After years and years of telling me that I was broken,
the cheap seats in the chapel were empty.
The power of the mother bear was that
she would soon be sleeping.

## CHILDHOOD LORE

That voice was a scar
that would soon stop bleeding.

## Red Mary-Janes

I'm just trying to get through the ugly hour.
Yet they ask me for the pretty word
that will dominate the next year.

I hope that girlhood will not die.
I am afraid it already has.

What can I say that will save me?
What can I say that will change me?
What word could shape a soft woman's body
into a palpable energy that can get me through the ugly hour?

I hope I go flying, like a house in Kansas.
I want to radiate pure magic,
like the witch that I crushed when I landed in Oz.

Red Mary-Janes are the only way home,
that home of girlhood, carried away in a basket.

I hope to be grown in a way that grows forever.
I hope to be loved like an ingénue—
benefit of the doubt to the naïve ones,
but harsher punishment for the least brainwashed.

I click my heels together, and I beg for some kind of balance.
Transitional glitter blankets my eyelashes—hopefully not
asbestos—
and I am back in a sepia-toned hug,
where no one will ever believe me.

## Dollhouse Downfall

I am a dollhouse,
inside of me are little versions of me
that exist and have their own passions, their own fears.
They are at war with each other—miniature swords and
cannons abound.
They cannot exist without cancelling each other out.

Every love they cherish exists only out of spite.
Each doll, their own universe, their own spirit.

Cotton balls in the bathtub make up bubbles,
origami wrappers as the wallpaper,
paper wreaths mounted at Christmas.
Each little detail is pretend.
It distracts the dolls from their differences.

But they are always still at war.
They refuse to see the beauty in each other.
And so they live in squalor.

Amidst clay Black Forest cake, with little red berries on top,
and a feather broom, a thimble bowl—
they use everything for everything, and yet they cannot see the
use
in each other.

Dollhouse downfall: a mind for everything, all at once.

## Plastic / Porcelain

You broke the china doll that sat in my old white hutch
when you threw a dagger in my direction.
Porcelain—pieces of my mind scatter across
the planks of the hardwood floor. They cut my feet
as I hope the dysfunction away.

I restrained myself for so long
in that cult of trees, its fruit that lied to me.
Now I suck the marrow of life out of the skin,
and my teeth twinge from the sweetness.

I miss the clarity I used to have,
brainwashed ease—I could know what was right
because I was told so. There was no test,
only blind obedience. And my mother taught me
that was love.

And so I loved you blindly,
without questioning the lily-white rage,
the screams, eggshell pandering. I obeyed
like you taught me to.

So that day when you broke the shelf,
everything collapsed—my delusions of you…
shattered. I picked up the pieces that fit,
and left behind the bloody remains.

The cult of trees cannot touch me now,
for I can see each root and its grasp within me.
The anxiety means nothing—

inherited trauma,
bestowed upon me. I can rewrite each word carved into my
bones,
and they will read as follows:

I am no one's victim. I am no one's possession.
I am skin and bone. I ache like a body that knows pain.
And you cannot take away how I got here. I am my own body.

Plastic and porcelain,
you cannot break me like that again.

## Wolf in Sheep's Wool

True monsters hurt those who have hurt none.
They create an enemy,
put on sheep's-wool clothing,
and bleat away about how they had just seen a wolf.

This disguise conceals the truth. True monsters twist the
truth's
core
to reveal something red and pulsing. It is living; it can feel pain.

They begin the war against the wolf, telling stories of its
mangy, corpse-like body—
its ferocious howl; it can be heard if you listen at the right time
of night…
It lurks around late to turn children into their victims.

But true monsters are those who hurt those who have nothing.
It's all a game.
True monsters hurt those who are already in pain.

They create an automatic response in your brain—
to be accustomed to the fear.
You better run; I hear the monsters behind, in my ears:

It's all a game—hide from the sick.
From the poor,
from the ugly,
from the loud, from the dicks,
from the roars
of wolves being held in cages.

Hide from the ones we believe belong in graves.
The world is full of monsters.
Maybe there is something worse at stake.
Howl—hide from what is fake.

## Tree Rings

I project our constellations onto the ceiling,
the one that tells the story of our first meeting.
It was destined by the stars that our minds would waltz until
midnight.

You are an artist;
you tell me all the grit and the beauty were forged to write the
lyrics
you whisper to me now.

The stars—
they fluttered to the forest floor, and underneath,
literary creatures came to visit you.
They told you stories of your greatness,
of your deal of sand and bone for ink in skin.

Quests for glory often require a payment of the flesh.

Each time I wake from my own story's nightmare,
this payment is made in the tree rings of trauma.
But the debt is paid. The art is made.

Like a skipping record,
I return for another dance.

**Marry or Martyr**

Suppose I kiss the skin
off your lips; in the passionate pain
you bleed onto mine.

As a little girl
I thought romance
was something special,
and I still try to—
but the cracks are red with blood,
and the heart is dead
when it breaks.

Some little girls dream of white fluffy dresses,
and some little girls dream of adventure without attachment.
There is little magic in knowing you are not a person
without a man present.

So how can we wish her a happily ever after
when she is being offered with a red ribbon around her neck?
A pretty prize to be devoured.
A petty man makes us his without another word.

When I was little,
I believed the champagne-frosted dream.
The spectacle of it all dazzled me—
a floral fantasy only afforded to the most romantic of notions.
This beautiful, nervous leap could not hinder even the hardest
of hearts.

I am afraid of the lies that are so often masqueraded in lace
and cream.
But cynics be damned,
I still believe in love.
I still believe in you.

**Flowers of Life**

Fertile womb, a place to grow,
a rotten flower
of delicate form—she dies.

Naïve, they called her,
after they left her red heart soaked
and painted her white. Sparks
burst from the little death
that would have killed her.

That's how she wanted to go,
in the middle.

Leaves grow from the lightning,
and she lives in the strikes.

## Rocking Chairs

I am so afraid—
of every joy going away,
of being seen as a useless spinster,
of being sick at such a young age.

I can't do anything of use.
I can't survive with this heavy noose
called time around my aching neck.

When I am with you, love feels light.
You don't make loving me into a chore.
When I'm with you, there's less angst to capture
and to write.
You make each dusty second less of a bore.

I want to seek asylum in an old dollhouse of my youth;
it sounds cozy, the thought is tempting
to my sentimental heart—felt, sewn with red and pink
thread—
to hide from time in your soft warm arms,

in our side-by-side rocking chairs,
as we grow old and not so afraid
all the time.

## Youth and Replaced

The moment where you see your youth so clearly,
from heaven or whatever stage play that was so moving—
and you hear that song play, the one that starts your life over,
and you are 18, suddenly 88, and your hands are grey.

Isn't that infinite moment of youth,
the titillating pleasure of being known—
isn't that how I feel when we are in each other's arms?

The thought of losing you,
the thought of growing old…
I'm afraid I might die young, and it aches inside
to fear never growing old together…

I made playlists when I was 15 about someone like you,
but I never thought I'd be lucky enough.
I sat next to this person I never knew,
and from that moment
we couldn't separate if we tried.

But there's this fear behind your eyes.
Growing old shouldn't bear such sorrows,
but the world likes expiration dates
as much as they like replacing anything old.

I know in wildflower graves I will be erased,
I will be replaced—
but it doesn't matter,
because in this life I knew you.

*Kate Gough*

## Sea Salt Tears

Pitch yourself.
You are cinnamon, baked by men with broken ovens, damaged
by neglect;
they bite into your warm, gooey centre.

When you speak, it soothes like chai—tear off a piece of bread
with a simple soup,
hearty, you are hot tea on a cold day,
and they sense it. They latch, like a leech; they cry to you,
but never ask you how your day was.

They only listen to recordings of old love songs,
never learning something new—only the same reassurance,
a soft hug from you in cashmere.

Taste the spice of life; a genius, a therapist, a poet, a lover—
they don't know it yet,
because they never listen.
They speak over you to get to know themselves.

Pitch yourself.
You are the mirror for the damaged soul
who has never known their—your—true self.

And they ask, What do you want?
Like they really care. And you talk about living by the sea—
and they interrupt you to talk about the ocean life they saw
when they were three.

# CHILDHOOD LORE

Empty pitcher and onion skin, peel back the layers in
the drought;
you have nothing left to give.

Cinnamon, sea salt tears—
you are more than a foil to me.

## The Language of Wildflowers

She layers my skin in baby's breath.
She kisses me, gives me all that I need.

Must this dried flower be a symbol for what you give to me?
Deflowered, press me into your pages; I am yours to keep.

I am bouquets of chamomile; you smell of me.
Pick wildflowers. You daren't take too many.
Not all stems are easy to press—some mould, some bulk,
some frail away in the heat.

A bouquet of humble ones—take the challenge
to tame the wild ones.

Press into the pages of a book
that smells of musky pulp and dusty ink;
perfume a poem that needn't any more pretty language.
Kiss the pages, with a weight of memory.
Store in a sun-soaked windowsill.

Once dry, label herbarium names at the bottom,
or sew them into valentines;
some violets are blue from being pressed flat
into a glass hanging frame.

In a book, or in the moor,
one in twenty flowers is yours to keep.

Be sensitive to nature,
and she will be preserved in the pages of the library.
Pick your flowers. Pick them carefully.
As they age, they will last
in your mind eternally.

Do not compare me to the flowers that dry.
I am perfume—muse at your wrist;
you remember me every time
you put on that silk dress of yours.

You try
not to think of that lingering scent.
But it brings you back.
And you think of me.

I now know my own colour.
Sewn into the pages,
I haunt myself with my own memory.

Pick me by the stem; I am yours to keep.
Wildflower, I am not fleeting.

## Seashell Cottages

The end is coming, and it is only just beginning.
It starts when the ivory and blue ceramic hands come to life,
and the sea of green irises watches back
with a heavy, blinking flutter.

Hollow home—I used to live near the ocean, and
in the sand we'd build seashell cottages for our dolls of kelp.

As girls, we'd make potions out of leaves and mud, and in the
back of our diary
was pressed the precious rose. She loved us back; her pages
wafted perfume
that made the whole library smell of rosewater.

As women, we'd collect our stories and put them in hope
chests, to one day
give to our daughters and their daughters. They taught us to
want it all.

But what happens when the doll
doesn't want it, and we are left with paper party hats
and glitter in our eye creases?
An empty birthday song fades from the balcony next over.

They are celebrating the day they were born. I cringe—
I wonder why I want to be loved and not feel sane?

The dolls taught us to want it all: picture-perfect,
cookie-cutter, plastic.
They want to be women, but what is a woman

—can you even tell?
What happens when wanting it all
leaves you with nothing?

## The Maidens of the Sea

Meet the lips
of the water maid, twinkle of the heart;
the moon blushes behind sapphic stars.

Knight in shining armour, hair of auburn and dusty brown—
long, shimmering strands never cut by the sword.
We shiver in the water, but our embrace is buttery in warmth.

Lovers, no longer hidden in the reeds—after years
of fear, the moon looks the same as the night we met.

Isolated prairies of ice and fire, oceans apart from
the maiden of the sea,
we could never meet.

Seas of sickness, smoky dragons,
and a fire swamp—a gothic quest in a suit of pearlescent
armour.
We fought through hell to be under the stars of our mothers.

This love was forged through the fog, and we will always be
a force to be reckoned with—
a love by the sea.

## Blink

When I opened my eyes, I saw it—
the white light they talk about.

Heavenly bodies, a starry way
to decorate ourselves;
adorned in lush twinkle, we shine
in order to speak.

I ask you,
"What will happen if I blink?"

You smile.
"It ends."

**Flowers in a Vase**

Isn't it funny how, when we see something pretty,
we pluck it from its roots and place it in a vase
to admire it in our own homes?

And yet this admiration
is what kills the flowers; they rot three days later…

When we listen to the radio,
and hear a song that inspires love,
we put it onto our playlists
and repeat it over and over until we no longer feel
anything when we hear it.

That beauty of a moment—
we repeat, repeat, repeat,
until the wonder is gone.

Isn't it funny how, when we love, that love can welt
like wildflowers in a vase?
They don't belong there;
they belong in the meadow.

I wonder,
why must we possess in order to love?

## Blue Powder Eyeshadow

*Joie de vivre* has left my corpse
to die a death so dull, my body hits the prairie floor with a
thud.

Forever promised to the winter-barren moor,
where I belong—my entire being belonging in icicled misery,
for evermore.

But what is this—? Is there not a second storm on the
horizon?
Not again. I muster the courage to dread tomorrow.
How can I go on with this lump
in my throat? On my wet black eyelashes, mascara I coat.

Blue powder eyeshadow
reminds the world of my chaos. Never have they seen a corpse
so chic;
they see the pathos in my physique,
and the image of the ingénue in a red babydoll dress
would forever shock them—
forever lock them up.

I lose my faith in their mercy
as they prove themselves faithless,
tasteless, in misery.

# Mushroom

Follow the moss,
lichen like breadcrumbs
we gather mushrooms.

Flesh rots, leave the bones;
we mould into a sunken grave.
The leaves crisp and crunch beneath foot.

Cradle in the woods, singing folklore gently,
grave by the sea, an elegy on the violin.

Follow the moss,
lichen like breadcrumbs
we rest in earth's tomb.

We pass on and grow from the womb,
into mushrooms.

## Mer-song of the Prairies

Rocky place in which I perch myself,
to brush my locks with a comb of shell,
and sing with her I call my kin.

Amelia—
she paints the skies and prairies
like the sea. Yellow straw makes up the tide
along the bales. We sing our siren songs
of folklore and tell-mores,
sea shores of wild rose and tumbleweed.

Mer-song of the Prairies;
a mermaid language
we keep to ourselves,
a song we hum as we
collect seaweed to feed the sheep.

Fluently, we wave back and forth
with the current;
we write our poems out as spells,
weighing in our hearts
as the
maidens of the sea.

# Pearl

Heal me, cover me, protect me from harm.
Relief comes in waves, as does the storm.
Ocean tides, salty skies,
I creak my bones in the water.

What's that, in the sand—
I see opalescence.

My mother once told me
a pearl is born from a wounded oyster.
Grains of sand penetrate its fragile shell,
and the oyster heals itself by coating the sand in nacre,
and after many layers and many moons,
it becomes a pearl.

The sparkle—the twinkle of stars inside me—
is seen only by the keen observer.

I am wounded.
From pain, I heal myself over and over,
and from that wound I grow a lace of jewels.

Mother of pearl, heal me close to your chest.
Safe and sound, I tie the pearls around my neck.

## The Circus Master

While the carousel horses gallop through her mind,
sugarplum miseries await her,
turning left at the end of dreamland
to an elephant graveyard
where the games are on.

She is a circus master
to the drum of her heartbeat.
A performance of pain
to the chucklers and groaners—
they chuck rotten tomatoes at her chin.

She is the main event, the golden goddess in a tiara of jewels,
she is the one they all came to see.

She falls ill in love, and they love to marvel at the stars.

Tonight the show must go on!
She takes the pills and fills her cup with tonic,
she is the star of the greatest show on earth.

The applause is a candle going out in a forest.

## Girlhood Prayer

Girlhood,
you were so cruel to me.
I always hoped for something kinder,
for a fallen angel to arrive and carry me home
from the pain, the hell I was in. To deliver me from sin.
The real kind, not the hypocrite's law, but the kind that
takes food from babies, takes homes away from the sick and
the suffering.

The kind of evil that warps everything in its path
and says they do it out of protection, for the young ones.
Where was my protection when I was young, or was it the
same
as the fear? The fear that they would find out my secret shame?
That I was raped, my girlhood stolen, but all Evil cared about
was my virginity. That protection — is that what you want?
For your babies to keep your secrets?
While you make more of them that won't have homes,
but at least you saved an egg, I guess. That's something.

I hope I get to be a girl today.
The boys — they get to be boys forever; adult men
are playing with toys, they just call them electronics.

I hope I get to be a girl who plays,
who eats ice cream and touches grass with her toes,
who gets dirty, and she doesn't need to keep her dress clean.
Even on Sundays. She is wild-eyed and beautiful,
but it doesn't hold her to any outside standard. She's the kind
of pretty

that makes you want to look more like yourself.
I hope to be like her one day.
I hope I get to be a girl today.

Girlhood,
you were an angel in disguise to me,
friendship found in the darkest places,
womanhood forged in the fire where we stood
the day I learned that no one was coming to save me.
You didn't save me.
But you taught me to save myself,
and for that,
I'll always be grateful.

## Childhood Lore

Pink satin dresses, ladybug necklaces, and ruby red slippers…
these are the fashionable relics of girlhood.
The lore of the little girl, the secret garden that prompts you to
speak to the robin perched atop
the ivy-strewn wall…
the pretty china doll that you learned to braid hair with…
the mystical lamp post you imagine will guide you to a faun in
a red knitted scarf, holding an
umbrella…

These memories make up a childhood.
These stories draw the map of the living.
Little girls create languages,
potions that cure the maladies,
legends that make us valiant,
a kingdom where we are all free to be ourselves fully.

Little girls are the keepers of ladylike folklore.
We recall our pain, love, and joy — it is written as we play.

## Tell Me a Fable from When You Were Small

Fairy tales are what we tell ourselves
and our children
as a prayer for happy endings
from our never-ending woes.
We hope for better.
We plead,
for the little ones, their fingers blue from picking berries
in the late August afternoon. They deserve the ever after.

We tell tales to hope for a better tomorrow,
we tell tales to cope with a bitter today.
Wide-eyed innocence, they see the just and the unjust
with such clarity.
Fairy tales of ugly ducklings, frost, and gingerbread cottages,
floral codes and wolves that howl when you greet them.

These are not just fanciful fables.
These are the stories we scrape together,
to understand the strange little world we live in.
They are the seeds that connect the children
to their wild forest roots.

Tell me a story, child.
Tell me a fable from when you were small.
Tell me a story that will give hope to us all.

## About the Author

Kate Gough is a Canadian-based poet (Treaty 7 region) and an active member of the online poetry community. Her work modernizes romantic literary sensibilities and explores recovery from trauma and the lived reality of chronic illness. She is drawn to fairy tales as the lore we tell ourselves in childhood — stories that help us build a reality sturdy enough to hold what is bigger and darker than we can comprehend. The folklore we pass down reveals who we are and who we dream of becoming; Gough hopes to mend those two worlds, to notice the beauty in life's humbler joys while still navigating the ever-painful present.

She has three poetry collections published by *Sunday Mornings at the River*, the most recent being *Dollhouse Downfall*. She has participated in the community poetry challenge *Escapril* six times, releasing new work every day for a month. Her writing has been featured in several poetry anthologies, including Sunday Mornings at the River's *It's Not Symptomatic, It's Systemic*. She has also taken part in local community projects such as *Disability Pride Alberta* and *YYC Portraits of People*.

Gough currently writes for *The Girlhood Project*. She hopes for a quiet, cozy life — often found with a cup of chamomile tea in hand. She can be found on Instagram and YouTube at @chamomilde.

## About the Press

Sunday Mornings at the River is an indie poetry press run by a neurodiverse working-class female poet. Its aim is to provide a home for poets outside the traditional publishing world.

Founded in 2012 by Rebecca Rijsdijk, Sunday Mornings at the River publishes poetry that names what others won't. Inspired by Salman Rushdie's belief that poetry should "name the unnamable, point at frauds, take sides," this is a space for work that doesn't look away. That resists silence. That makes itself heard—whether through grief, anger, hope, or all of the above.

The press centre voices long ignored by the literary world: working-class poets, women, people living with illness, and anyone who got told their stories were too raw, too much, or not enough.

Scan me
for more books
by Sunday Mornings
at the River

w: sundaymorningsattheriver.com
e: hello@sundaymorningsattheriver.com
ig: @sundaymorningsattheriver